Read Stories – Learn English

The Hound of the Baskervilles

by Sir Arthur Conan Doyle

CEFR level A1+

**Adapted by Karen Kovacs
for
Read Stories – Learn English**

Read Stories – Learn English

The Hound of the Baskervilles: CEFR level A1+ (ELT Graded Reader)
Original text by Sir Arthur Conan Doyle
Adapted text © Karen Kovacs, 2024
Logo © Karen Kovacs, 2024

No part of this book may be reproduced, scanned or distributed in any printed or electronic form without permission. Please do not participate in or encourage piracy of copyrighted materials in violation of the author's rights. Thank you for respecting the hard work of the author.

CONTENTS

What are graded readers?	Page 8
Meet the author	Page 9
People in the story	Page 11
The story	Page 13
More stories	Page 64
Words from the story	Page 66

WHAT ARE GRADED READERS?

Graded readers are books in easy English. They are written for learners of English and they have **vocabulary and grammar at your level**.

Each book has some new, more difficult words. There are **definitions** for these words at the back of the book.

WHY READ GRADED READERS?

- Studies show that learners who read in English **improve in all areas much more quickly** than learners who don't read.

- With graded readers, you **don't need a dictionary** so reading is more **relaxing**.

- The stories are all in **modern English**.

- You can learn vocabulary and grammar **in context** (this is the best way, according to teachers).

- Reading a book in English will improve your **comprehension**, your **fluency** and your **confidence**.

- The stories are **exciting** and reading them is **fun**!

Meet
the author

My name is Karen.

- I was born and brought up in England.
- I have a Master's degree in Linguistics.
- I have a teaching diploma and many years' teaching experience in the UK and abroad.
- I've written lots of books for learners of English.
- I speak Hungarian, French and Spanish so I understand what it's like to learn a foreign language!

Karen Kovacs

ReadStories-LearnEnglish.com

Other stories at the same level

New words

When you see a word in **bold**, go to the back of the book. There you will find a definition of the word.

People in the story

Sherlock Holmes

Dr Watson

Henry Baskerville

Dr Mortimer

Mr and Mrs Barrymore

Jack Stapleton

Miss Stapleton

The Hound of the Baskervilles

CHAPTER 1

Sherlock Holmes often woke up late in the mornings, but today he was at the breakfast table early. When I came into the room, he looked up.

"Good morning, Watson," he said. "A man is coming to see us today."

"Does he need our help?" I asked.

"Yes," he answered. "His name is Dr Mortimer."

A short time later, the doctor came into the room. He was a tall, thin man with a long nose, and he wore glasses.

"Mr Holmes, I have a big problem," he said. "I came to you because you're the second-best **detective** in Europe!"

"Oh, am I?" said Holmes slowly. "Please tell me, who is the best?"

Dr Mortimer looked at Holmes's face. The detective was angry. The doctor waited before answering.

"Erm … uh …," he began, "Mr Bertillon, I think. People say that."

"Oh, do they?" asked Holmes. "Then ask Mr Bertillon for help, not me."

"No, no!" said Dr Mortimer quickly. "I would like *your* help! I'm sorry – did I make you angry?"

"Yes, a little," answered Holmes. "But don't worry. Please sit down."

We all sat down, and then Holmes said, "This is my friend, Dr Watson."

"Good morning," Dr Mortimer said.

"How can we help you?" I asked him.

"Before I tell you," he said, "can I ask you something?"

"Of course," Holmes said.

"Do you know the story of the **Hound** of the Baskervilles?"

"I'm too old for stories, Dr Mortimer," said the detective.

"Please listen to it," said the doctor. "It's important."

"Alright," said Holmes, and he closed his

eyes. He often did this when he listened to people.

"The Baskervilles are a very old, **rich** family," he began. "They live in Devon and they have a big house on the **moor**. It's called Baskerville Hall. In the 1600s, Hugo Baskerville lived there. He loved a woman from a poor family but she didn't want him."

"Why not?" I asked.

"Because he was an **evil** man," said Dr Mortimer, "and she was **scared** of him. But, one day, Hugo went to her family's house in the village and he said, 'You're coming with me to Baskerville Hall!' He put her in one of the bedrooms and he told her, 'You can never leave!'"

The doctor stopped talking and he looked at Holmes. His eyes were closed. "Is he sleeping?" Dr Mortimer asked me.

Holmes heard him and he said, "I'm listening to every word."

"What did the woman do?" I asked Dr Mortimer.

"The window was small," he said, "but she was very thin. One night, she opened it and she **jumped** out. She ran onto the moor. Hugo went to her bedroom but she wasn't there."

"Was he angry?" I asked.

"Yes, very!" said Dr Mortimer. "He had lots of hounds. 'Find that woman!' he told them. 'She left me and now she must die!' The dogs all ran onto the moor. They **howled** and howled. Hugo went too, on his black horse."

"Did they find her?" I said.

"No," said the doctor. "The hounds stopped running because they were scared of something. They went back home. But two men from the village found the woman's body. Close to it, there was the body of Hugo. 'Look!' one of the men said. 'A hound is eating his body!'"

"Was it one of Hugo's hounds?" I asked.

"No," the doctor answered. "Hugo's hounds

were white. But this hound was big and black, and **fire** came from its mouth! After that night, every man from the Baskerville family dies on the moor."

The doctor looked at Holmes and waited. After a minute, Holmes slowly opened his eyes. "That's an interesting story ... for children."

Dr Mortimer walked to Holmes's chair. "Look!" he said and he showed the detective a newspaper. "Charles Baskerville lived at Baskerville Hall. I was his doctor and his friend. On 14 May this year, he died ... on the moor."

"I see," said Holmes. "Why was he on the moor at night?"

"We don't know," said the doctor.

"Did a **supernatural** hound with fire in its mouth eat his body?" asked Holmes, but he **smiled** when he said it.

"No," said Dr Mortimer.

"Why did he die?" I asked.

"He had a problem with his heart, didn't he?"

said Holmes.

"Yes!" answered the doctor. "How did you know?"

"Charles knew the story of the Hound of the Baskervilles," Holmes said. "He heard a howl, I think – one of the village dogs. He was scared and his heart stopped."

"But ..." began the doctor.

"Yes?" said Holmes. "What is it?"

"Near his body," said the doctor, "there were ... **footprints**."

"Footprints?" asked Holmes. "A man's or a woman's?"

Dr Mortimer looked at us. Then he said, very slowly, "They were the footprints of a big hound!"

CHAPTER 2

CHAPTER 2

Holmes thought for a minute or two. We waited. Then he asked the doctor, "Is a new Baskerville man coming to live at the Hall?"

"Yes," he answered. "His name is Henry Baskerville. Charles had no children. Henry is the son of Charles's younger brother. He's the last Baskerville in the family." The doctor put his hand on Holmes's arm and he said, "I'm very scared! Henry will die on the moor too – I know it! Please help!"

"Where is this man?" asked the detective.

"He lived on a farm in Canada," said the doctor, "but he's coming to London today. In two or three days, he'll go to Baskerville Hall, his new home."

"Come here tomorrow with him."

"I will. Thank you!" said the doctor.

The next day, Dr Mortimer and Henry Baskerville came to the flat. Holmes and I said hello to him. Henry was a small man with dark hair, about thirty years old.

"Why are we here?" he asked. "Dr Mortimer didn't tell me. How can I help you?"

"We want to help *you*," answered Holmes.

"But I don't need help," said Henry.

"Do you know the story of the Hound of the Baskervilles?" asked the detective.

"Of course," said Henry. "But it's only a story. Dogs don't have fire in their mouths!"

"No, they don't," said Holmes. "But the moor is not a safe place for you. **Someone** ... or something ... is **killing** the Baskerville men. We don't understand it but we'll find the answer."

"Yes, alright," said Henry. "But I can't stay here any longer now. Dr Mortimer and I are hungry and we need some breakfast. We're going to a café."

The men left but Holmes watched them from the window.

"What are you doing?" I asked my friend.

"Look, Watson," he said. "There is a taxi in

the street."

I didn't understand. "There are always taxis in the street, Holmes. Why are you watching it?"

"Henry and Dr Mortimer are walking down the street and the taxi is **following** them," he said.

"Oh, is it?" I said, **surprised**.

"Someone is watching Henry!" Holmes said.

We left the flat and we ran into the street. We followed the taxi.

In the back, there was a man with a black beard. "Who is he?" I asked Holmes.

"I don't know," he answered.

Then the man saw us. "Oh no!" said Holmes. The next second, the taxi drove quickly down the street and we couldn't see it.

That evening, we met with the two men again.

"Someone followed you this morning from this flat," Holmes told them.

"What?" asked Henry. He was surprised. "Who was it?"

"We don't know," answered Holmes. "He had a black beard."

"Charles Baskerville's **servant** has a black beard," said Dr Mortimer.

"What's the servant's name?" said Holmes.

"Barrymore. But he's not in London," the doctor said. "He's at Baskerville Hall. He and his wife live and work there."

"Barrymore found Charles's body, is that right?" he asked.

"Yes, he did," said the doctor.

Holmes thought for a minute and then he asked, "When Charles died, did the Barrymores get any money?"

"Yes," Dr Mortimer answered. "They got five hundred pounds each."

Holmes looked at the doctor. "And you?"

"Me?" he said.

"You don't want to tell me." Holmes smiled.

"It's alright. I'll tell you," answered Dr Mortimer. "I got a thousand pounds."

"I see," said Holmes.

"And I got seven hundred thousand pounds and Baskerville Hall," Henry told us. "I'm going there tomorrow for the first time. I'm so excited."

"My friend, Dr Watson, will go with you," said Holmes. "There is the story of the hound and now someone is following you. You're not safe. Watson will stay with you at the house. And never go onto the moor **alone**!"

"You're not coming?" I asked my friend.

"No, Watson," he answered. "I have lots of work here in London."

"Oh," I said sadly.

"When you're at Baskerville Hall," he told me later, "talk to the servants and to the people in the village. Ask them about Charles Baskerville and about this supernatural hound. Write to me with any new information."

CHAPTER 3

From the window of the train, Henry Baskerville saw the moor.

"The sun is going down," he said, "and the moor looks beautiful but also dark and **scary**."

We got off at a small station, and we started travelling on the moor. "In half an hour, you'll see your new home," Dr Mortimer said to Henry.

We saw a policeman on the moor. "Why is he here?" asked Henry.

"A man **escaped** from **prison** last week," Dr Mortimer said. "The police are looking for him. They're watching the moor, and also every station and every road."

We didn't speak for five minutes. There was a cold wind and it was darker now.

"Where did Hugo Baskerville die?" I asked Dr Mortimer.

"He died there, the story says." He showed us the place on the moor.

"And Charles Baskerville?" asked Henry.

"He died there." Dr Mortimer showed us a

different place. My body went cold.

A minute later, we saw a very big, old house in the centre of the moor. "Is that my new home?" Henry asked.

"Yes, it is," answered Dr Mortimer.

A tall man with a black beard came out of the dark house. "Welcome to Baskerville Hall!" he said. "I'm Barrymore."

Behind him, there was a woman. She didn't smile.

"Is that your wife?" asked Henry.

"Yes," said the servant. "This is Mrs Barrymore."

Dr Mortimer went back to his house in the village, and Henry and I went into Baskerville Hall.

There were lots of pictures of the Baskerville family. The men and women looked down at us from the walls.

Henry wasn't very happy with his new home, I could see. "Let's go to bed early tonight," he said. "In the morning light, the house will be nicer."

We went up to our bedrooms and I got into bed.

I didn't sleep very well. At about two o'clock in the morning, I heard a noise. "A woman is **crying**," I thought. I waited for thirty minutes but I heard no other noise. I went back to sleep.

The next morning, Henry and I ate breakfast together in the dining room. Sunlight came in the windows.

"How do you feel about the house this morning, Henry?" I asked.

"I like it!" he answered. "I didn't like it last night because I was tired and cold. But I feel better today."

"Did you hear a woman in the night?" I said.

"Yes, I did," he said. "Who was it?"

Before I could answer, Barrymore, the servant, came into the room. Henry asked him about the noise.

"There are only two women in the house," answered Barrymore, "my wife and a young servant girl. The noise didn't come from my wife. She didn't cry last night."

But this wasn't **true**.

After breakfast, I saw Mrs Barrymore. Her eyes were red.

CHAPTER 4

Later, I sat at the desk in my bedroom and I thought, "Barrymore found Charles's body. He and his wife got some money when Charles died. A man with a black beard followed Henry in London. And now, his wife is crying in the night. What shall I do?"

I remembered the young servant girl. "I know!" I thought. "I'll speak to her."

I found her in the kitchen. "Tell me," I said, "did Mr Barrymore leave Baskerville Hall last week? Did he go to London?"

"No, no," she said. "Mr Barrymore never leaves Baskerville Hall. He and his wife are always here."

Was this true? I didn't know.

It was a beautiful day and I went for a walk on the moor. After twenty minutes, I heard someone behind me.

I looked and I saw a small, thin man, about thirty-five years old. "Why is this man following me?" I thought.

"Good morning, Dr Watson," he said with a smile. "My name is Jack Stapleton and I live at Merripit House. It's near here."

"How do you know my name?" I asked.

"Dr Mortimer told me about you," he answered, "and I wanted to meet you."

"I see," I said.

"Does Henry Baskerville like his new home?" he asked.

"Yes, he does," I said.

We started walking together. After two or three minutes, he asked me, "Do you know the story of the supernatural hound?"

"Yes," I said.

"The people from the village sometimes see a big dog on the moor," Stapleton said.

"Do they?" I asked. "But how is that possible? The story isn't true."

He didn't answer me. A minute or two later, he said, "You work with Sherlock Holmes, don't you? Is he here with you?"

"No, he isn't," I told him. "He has lots of important work in London."

I heard a noise. "What is that?" I asked.

"A moor horse is crying because it's dying," answered Stapleton. "It's in the **marsh**."

"What's the marsh?" I asked.

"It's a part of the moor," Stapleton said. "It's not safe – for horses or people. When someone goes into the marsh, their body goes down, down, down. They can never escape."

I heard the horse again and my body went cold. The moor was a scary place.

Stapleton stopped and he asked, "Would you like to meet my sister? Our house is very near here, on the moor."

We walked to his house together. It was small and ugly.

There, I met Miss Stapleton. She was tall, thin and beautiful, with dark hair. Her brother went into a different room and she came close to me.

She looked into my eyes and she said, "Go

back to London!"

"What?" I asked. "Why?"

"I can't tell you," she said quickly. "But you must leave and never come back."

Her brother came back into the room. "What are you and Dr Watson talking about?" he asked his sister.

"Dr Watson?" she said, very surprised. Then she looked at me. "You're not Henry Baskerville?"

"No, I'm not," I answered.

"Oh!" she said. She sat down and she didn't speak again.

CHAPTER 5

Some time later, I wrote a letter to Holmes in London with all the new information. At the end, I wrote:

"Henry Baskerville and I went to Merripit House for lunch last week. Miss Stapleton is a beautiful and clever woman. Henry loves her very much, I think. We see the Stapletons often, and Henry and Miss Stapleton talk for hours.

"One day, Mr Stapleton got very angry with Henry. 'You love my sister, don't you?' he said. 'But she can never be your wife!'

"Henry is a good and rich man, and he loves Stapleton's sister. Why is that a problem?

"I asked Miss Stapleton and she said, 'My brother has no family, only me. When I'm Henry's wife, I'll leave Merripit House and my brother will be alone.'

"They have to wait for three months, Stapleton says, and then they can be husband

and wife."

That night, at two o'clock in the morning, I heard a noise outside my bedroom door. I opened it and I saw Barrymore!

He didn't see me and I followed him. He went into a room in a different part of the house. He stood at the window and he looked at the dark moor.

I went quickly to Henry's bedroom. "Wake up!" I said. "Come with me." We went back to the room and we watched Barrymore.

After five minutes, Henry said to him, "What are you doing, Barrymore?"

The servant looked at us and his face went white. "Nothing," he answered.

"That's not true, is it?" said Henry.

He gave us a different answer now. "I can't tell you," he said.

"Do you do this every night?" Henry asked. Barrymore didn't answer. "You're my servant," said Henry, "but you don't answer my questions. Tomorrow, you can find a new job, and your wife too!"

"I'm so sorry!" someone said behind us in the dark room. We looked and we saw Mrs Barrymore. "My husband is doing nothing bad," she told us. "My brother is ..." She stopped talking and she started crying.

I finished her sentence. "Your brother is the man on the moor. We heard about him. He escaped from prison."

"Yes, that's right," said Mrs Barrymore. "My little brother killed someone and he went to prison. He escaped and now he's living on the moor. I love him so much and I want to help him. Every night, we wait for him. When he comes, we go down and we give him food."

"But he killed someone! You mustn't help him!" said Henry, very angry. "It's not safe. Miss Stapleton isn't safe! He **might** kill her!"

"No, no, he won't! He wants to go to South

America and start a new life. He'll be ready in a day or two. Then he'll leave England and he'll never come back," said Mrs Barrymore. "He won't kill again."

"We don't know that!" said Henry. Then, to me, he said, "Come with me, Watson. Let's find this man."

We left Baskerville Hall and we ran onto the dark moor. We started looking for Mrs Barrymore's brother.

Then we heard a noise. It was a howl.

I looked behind me and I saw Henry's face. It was very white.

He put his hand on my arm. "What was that, Watson?" he said.

"I don't know," I answered. "The village people often hear howling on the moor."

"Watson," said Henry, "it was the howl of a hound."

My body went cold and I couldn't speak.

"What do the village people say about the

noise?" asked Henry. I didn't want to answer him but he said, "Tell me, Watson!"

"It's the howl of the Hound of the Baskervilles, they say."

He didn't speak for a minute, then he said, "Is the story true, do you think?"

"No, of course not," I answered. "But shall we go back to the house?"

"No!" he said. "We have to find that **prisoner**."

Ten minutes later, we saw him. He had a dark beard and small, dark eyes. When he saw us, he ran really quickly and he escaped.

We started walking back to Baskerville Hall when I saw a second man, about one hundred metres from us. He was tall and thin but I couldn't see his face.

"Look!" I said to Henry. "Who is that?"

"Who are you talking about?" Henry said. I looked again but the man was gone. Was he supernatural?

CHAPTER 6

The next morning, I wrote to Holmes about the Barrymores. Then I walked on the moor. I wanted to find that man again. Who was he? He was taller than Stapleton. It might be Barrymore but he was always at Baskerville Hall.

I looked for an hour, but I didn't see the man.

That evening, Barrymore brought me some coffee in my bedroom. "Has your wife's brother gone now?" I asked him.

"I don't know," he said. "I put some food under a tree for him on Tuesday. I didn't see him but, the next day, the food wasn't there. The other man took it, I think."

I looked at him. "The other man?"

"Yes," Barrymore answered. "There is a second man. There are old houses on the moor. They are thousands of years old, without doors or windows. That man lives in one of them and a boy from the village takes him food."

When the servant left, I stood at the window and I looked into the black night. It was very cold and windy, and I thought, "How can a man live on the moor in this weather?"

Before dinner the next day, I went back onto the moor and I looked for the old houses.

After an hour, I found them. Inside one of the houses, there was some food on the floor. And there was also a pen and paper.

Then I heard a noise outside. "He's coming!" I thought. I waited, very scared.

"It's a beautiful day, my friend," someone said.

I looked and I saw Holmes!

He smiled at me. "You're surprised," he said.

"Yes, I am! What are you doing here?"

"I wanted to watch you and Henry. The moor isn't a safe place," he told me. "I was here all the time but I didn't want people to know that."

"Why not?" I asked. "Is it because you're famous?"

"Yes," he said. "We need to find the killer.

But with a famous detective here, the killer might leave."

He knew all the new information. Someone in London sent him all my letters.

"I have some new information for *you*," Holmes told me. "Charles Baskerville was on the moor that night because he wanted to meet a woman. Her name is Laura Lyons and she lives near here."

"Why did he meet her?" I asked.

"He didn't," Holmes said. "She never came."

"Oh."

"In a letter, Laura asked him for money," Holmes said. "Charles was rich and he often gave people money."

"Did Charles love her?" I asked.

"I don't know," said Holmes, "but *she* didn't love *him*."

"How do you know that?"

"Because she loves Stapleton," he told me. "They meet ... they write ... But Stapleton doesn't love Laura. He has a wife."

"A wife? Who?" I asked.

"Miss Stapleton is not his sister," Holmes said. "She's his wife. She's Mrs Stapleton."

"What?" I was very surprised. "Stapleton never told us that. Why not?" I asked.

Holmes thought for a minute. "Stapleton told Laura, 'Write a letter to Charles Baskerville about meeting on the moor.' She did it because she loves Stapleton and she doesn't know about his wife. Then he told her, 'Don't meet him.' Charles waited alone on the moor for Laura. Stapleton went and he killed him."

"I see," I said.

"And," Holmes said, "Henry Baskerville loves Mrs Stapleton and he goes often to Merripit House. This helps Stapleton because he wants to kill Henry. One day, he will invite Henry to the house and he will kill him."

"He's an evil man," I said.

"He also followed Henry Baskerville in

London," Holmes said. "It was him in the taxi."

"How is that possible?" I asked. "Stapleton doesn't have a beard."

"It was a **fake** beard," Holmes said.

"Oh, I see." I thought for a minute. "But why does Stapleton want to kill the Baskerville men?" I asked.

"I don't know," Holmes said. "But we must watch him."

The sun was gone now, and it was dark and cold. Then we heard a **scream**!

"Oh no!" I said. "Where is that noise coming from?"

We listened and we heard a second scream. "It's nearer now," said Holmes. His face was white. He was never scared but, tonight, for the first time, he was.

Then we heard a different sound – a howl.

"Quickly, come with me!" said Holmes. "It's the hound! It's killing Henry!"

CHAPTER 7

Holmes started running and I followed him. We heard a third scream and then nothing.

"We're too late," said Holmes.

It was very dark and we couldn't see much but we ran and ran.

Then Holmes saw something on the floor and he stopped. It was a man's body but we couldn't see his face.

"Oh no," Holmes said. "It's Henry."

We were both very sad and also very scared. Where was the hound? Did he kill Henry and then leave? And where was Stapleton?

I looked down at the body and I said to Holmes, "Wait! This man has a beard! It's not Henry!"

"What?" Holmes said, surprised.

"It's Mrs Barrymore's brother, the prisoner!" I told him.

Holmes looked at the man's face. "You're right," he said. "The hound killed the wrong person."

We heard a noise and we felt scared again. Then we saw Stapleton.

"Don't talk to him about the hound," Holmes told me quickly.

When Stapleton saw the body, he said, "Is that Henry Baskerville?"

"No," Holmes said. "It's the prisoner."

Stapleton's face went white. "Oh," he said sadly. Then he looked at us and he said, "I invited Henry for dinner but he didn't come. Then I heard a scream and I thought, 'Oh no, it's Henry! I must help him!'"

Stapleton looked at my friend and he said, "You're Sherlock Holmes, aren't you? Are you staying here for long?"

"No," Holmes answered. "I'm leaving tomorrow." Of course, this wasn't true.

We talked more and then Stapleton left. We wanted to carry the body home but it was too difficult. We put it in one of the old houses on the moor and we started walking back to

Baskerville Hall.

When we got back the house, Henry was in the living room. We didn't tell him about Stapleton and the hound. We needed more information first.

"Stapleton invited me to Merripit House this evening," Henry told us. "I wanted to go but I didn't. You told me, 'Never go onto the moor at night alone.'"

"Well done," I said.

"Yes, well done," said Holmes. "We're very …" He stopped talking and looked at the wall.

"What is it?" we both said.

The detective smiled. "The people in those pictures are your family. Is that right?"

"Yes, that's right," Henry answered. "The first picture is Hugo. He started the Hound of the Baskervilles."

Henry went to bed, and Holmes and I stayed in the room.

Holmes looked again at the wall. "Look at the picture of Hugo, Watson. The face is the same as Stapleton's."

"Stapleton?" I said. "Oh, you're right! The two men have the same nose and eyes."

"Stapleton is a Baskerville!" Holmes said. "He wants to kill Henry and get his money and this house!"

CHAPTER 8

The next morning, at breakfast, we talked to Henry.

"You're going to Merripit House this evening, is that right?" Holmes asked him.

"Yes, Stapleton invited me," he answered.

"We won't come with you," Holmes said. He saw Henry's surprised face and he said, "Don't ask any questions. Go for dinner with the Stapletons and have fun."

"Erm, alright," said Henry, but he was very scared.

That evening, Henry had dinner with the Stapletons, and Holmes and I waited outside outside the house in the dark.

"What are we waiting for?" I asked.

"You'll see," Holmes said.

After two hours, Henry and Stapleton came out of the house. Dinner was finished. Mrs Stapleton wasn't with them. They said goodbye and Henry started walking home alone. He didn't see us.

Then Stapleton went to the back of the house and he opened the door to a small room. Something came out of the room. It was a dog.

It was really big and fire came from its mouth. It ran onto the moor. "It's following Henry," said Holmes.

Henry looked back and he saw the hound. He started screaming. The next second, Henry was on the floor and the evil hound jumped on him!

Holmes ran to Henry and the dog. The dog opened its mouth. "It's going to eat him!" I said. But quickly, Holmes took a knife from his coat and he killed the dog with it.

Henry's face was white. "What was that?" he said.

"I don't know but I killed it," said Holmes. "That's the end of the story of the Hound of the Baskervilles."

We all looked at the dog. It was not supernatural but it was very, very big.

Holmes looked inside the hound's mouth. "Stapleton put a **chemical** in its mouth," he said, "and the chemical made a fake fire."

"Why did he do that?" I asked.

"It made people scared of the dog," Holmes told me. "People saw the fire and they thought, 'It's the hound from the story.'"

"Where is Stapleton?" I said.

"Good question," said Holmes.

We looked for him in the house. We couldn't find him but we found his wife. She was in one of the bedrooms and the door was closed. "My husband put me in here and I couldn't leave," she told us when we opened the door. "I wanted to tell you about the hound but I couldn't."

We couldn't look for Stapleton on the moor in the dark. It wasn't safe. We took Henry back to Baskerville Hall and we told him about the Stapletons. Of course, he was very surprised.

The next morning, we went onto the moor and

we found Stapleton's footprints. They stopped at the marsh.

"Ah, I see," said Holmes. "Stapleton ran into the marsh last night and he died."

Mrs Stapleton told us about her husband. He was the son of Rodger Baskerville. Rodger was the youngest brother of Charles Baskerville. He went to live in South America and the family never knew about his son.

Rodger died and Jack Baskerville changed his name to Stapleton. He and his wife came to live at Merripit House. He wanted Baskerville Hall and the money, but first he had to kill Charles and then Henry. He bought a black dog and, with its help, he killed Charles, but he couldn't kill Henry.

After that night, Henry felt sad and scared for a long time. Yesterday, he left the country with Dr Mortimer – they're going on a long holiday together. That might help him and, one day, he might be happy again.

Get a free story and free exercises for this book

Go to **ReadStories-LearnEnglish.com** and enter your email address.

You will get a **free story** and **exercises** for each of my books (vocabulary exercises, comprehension exercises and notes about British culture).

You will also get news about my new books.

MORE STORIES

A1+ Elementary

A2 Pre-intermediate

B1 Intermediate

B2 Upper intermediate

Words from the story

alone (adj)
without any other people

angry (adj)
having strong feelings about something that you dislike very much

chemical (n)
a substance or liquid that creates a reaction

cry (v)
produce tears because you are unhappy

detective (n)
a person who investigates crimes and catches criminals

escape (v)
get away from a place where you have been kept as a prisoner or not allowed to leave

evil (adj)
enjoying harming others; morally bad

fake (adj)
not real

fire (n)
the flames, light and heat that something makes when it burns

follow (v)
go behind somebody / something; go after somebody because you want to watch where they go

footprint (n)
a mark from a person's foot or shoe or an animal's foot

hound (n)
a dog that can run fast and has a good sense of smell, used for hunting

howl (v)
(of a dog or wolf) make a long, loud call (**howl**, n)

jump (v)
move quickly off the ground or away from a surface by pushing yourself with your legs and feet

kill (v)
make somebody die (**killer** – person, n)

marsh (n)
an area of low land that is always soft and wet because the water can't leave

might (modal v)
used when showing that something is or was possible

moor (n)
an open area of hills covered with rough grass, especially in Britain

prison (n)
a building where the police keep criminals (**prisoner** – person, n)

rich (adj)
having a lot of money

scared (adj)
afraid that something bad might happen (**scary** – making someone feel scared, adj)

scream (n)
a loud high shout made by somebody who is hurt or scared (**scream**, v)

servant (n)
a person who works in another person's house, and cooks, cleans etc for them

smile (v)
when you are happy and the corners of your mouth turn up (**smile**, n)

someone (pro)
a person who is not known or mentioned by name

supernatural (adj)
that cannot be explained by the laws of science and that seems to involve gods or magic

surprised (adj)
feeling surprise because something happened that you did not expect

true (adj)
right and not wrong; a fact

www.ingramcontent.com/pod-product-compliance
Lightning Source LLC
Chambersburg PA
CBHW011959090526
44590CB00023B/3785